CHURCH SOLOS FOR KIDS

Arranged by Joel Matthys

CONTENTS

Children Singers: [1]Amanda Addison, age 12.   [2]Martin Bourqui, age 10.
[3]Katharine Chambers, age 12.   [4]Katie Chu, age 9.   [5]Amber Edmunds, age 12.
[6]Caroline Straty, age 9.   [7]Claire Straty, age 7.

Recorded at Dallas Sound Lab, 9/20/97.
Singers prepared by Louise Lerch at The Meadows School of the Arts, Southern Methodist University.

To access companion recorded performances
and accompaniments online, visit:
www.halleonard.com/mylibrary

Enter Code
3644-5951-5810-9280

ISBN 978-0-7935-8228-0

Visit Hal Leonard Online at
www.halleonard.com

Contact us:
Hal Leonard
7777 West Bluemound Road
Milwaukee, WI 53213
Email: info@halleonard.com

In Europe, contact:
Hal Leonard Europe Limited
42 Wigmore Street
Marylebone, London, W1U 2RN
Email: info@halleonardeurope.com

In Australia, contact:
Hal Leonard Australia Pty. Ltd.
4 Lentara Court
Cheltenham, Victoria, 3192 Australia
Email: info@halleonard.com.au

T0055380

AMAZING GRACE

Words by JOHN NEWTON
Music by VIRGINIA HARMONY

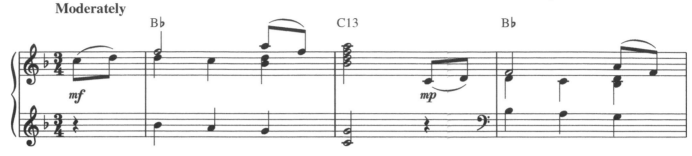

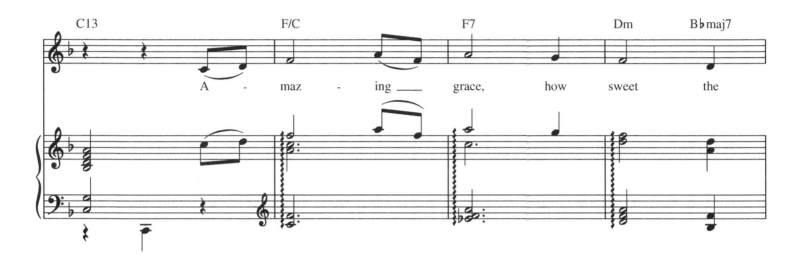

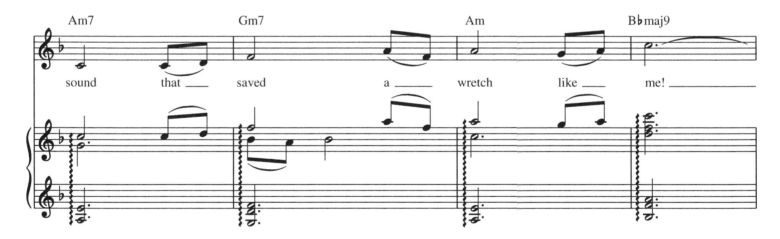

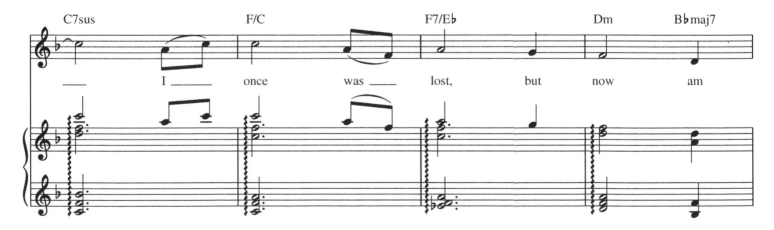

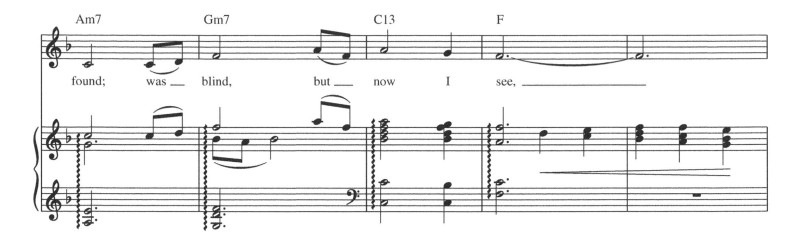

found; was __ blind, but __ now I see, _____

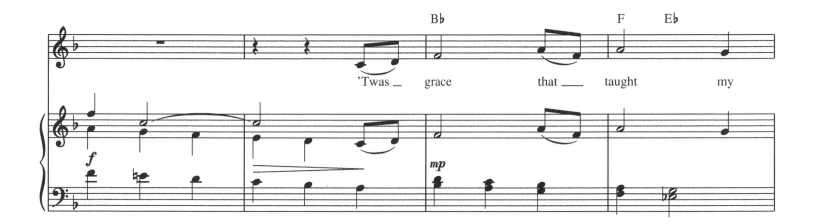

'Twas __ grace that __ taught my

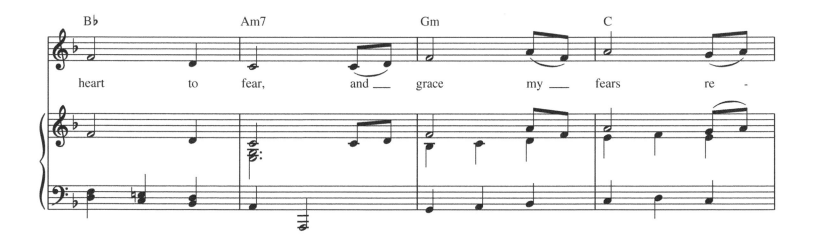

heart to fear, and __ grace my __ fears re -

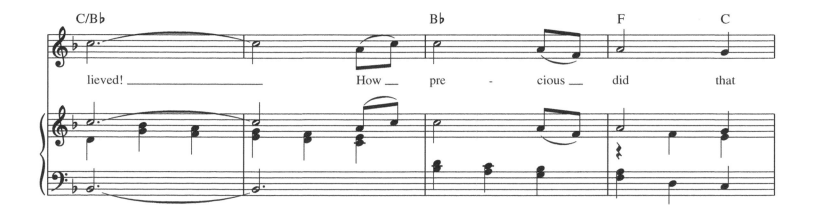

lieved! _____ How __ pre - cious __ did that

grace ap - pear the ___ hour I ___ first be -

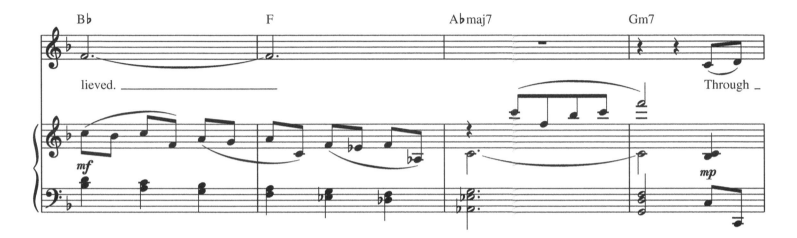

lieved. _____ Through _ man -

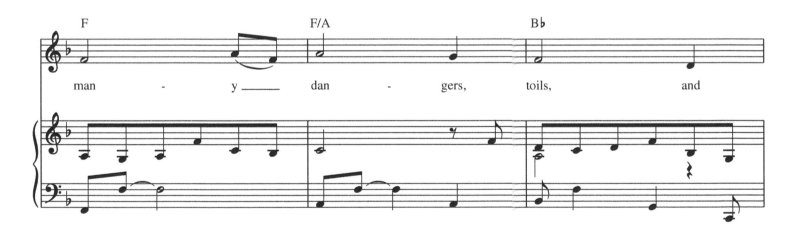

man - y ___ dan - gers, toils, and

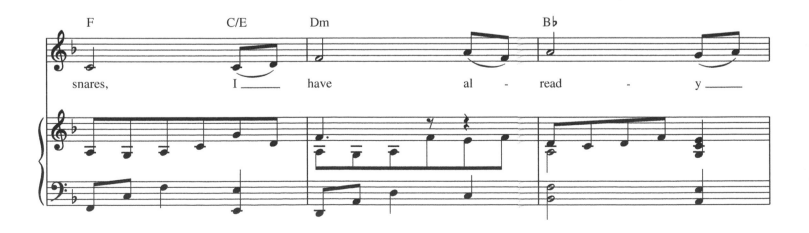

snares, I ___ have al - read - y ___

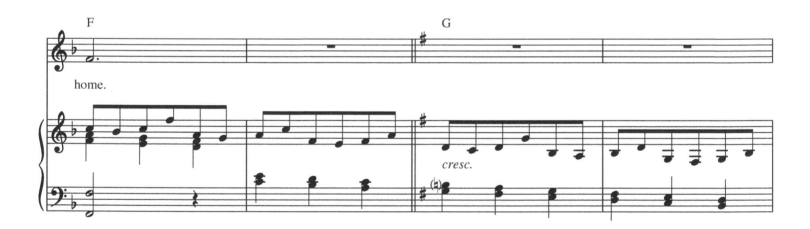

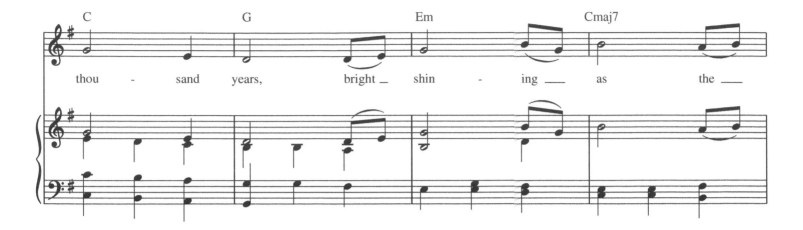

thou - sand years, bright __ shin - ing __ as the __

sun, _____ we've __ no less __ days to

sing God's praise than __ when we'd __ first be -

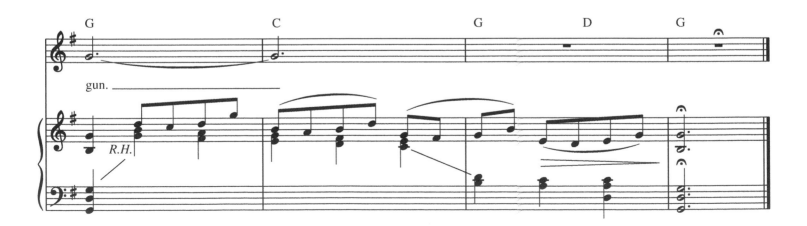

gun. _____

DOWN IN MY HEART

Traditional

Quick and energetic!

peace that pass-eth un-der-stand-ing down in my heart down in my heart

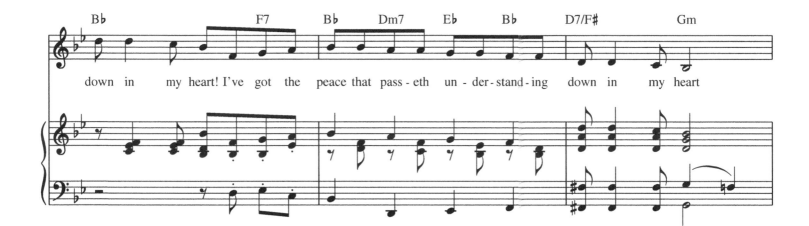

down in my heart! I've got the peace that pass-eth un-der-stand-ing down in my heart

down in my heart to stay!

I've got the

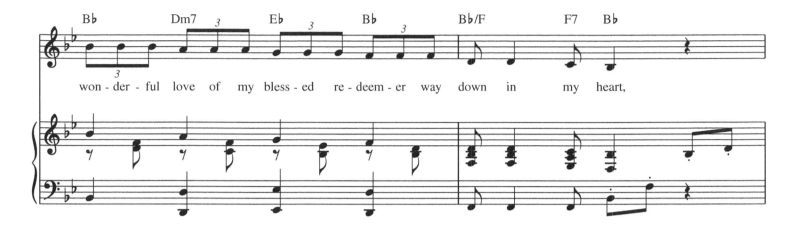

won-der-ful love of my bless-ed re-deem-er way down in my heart,

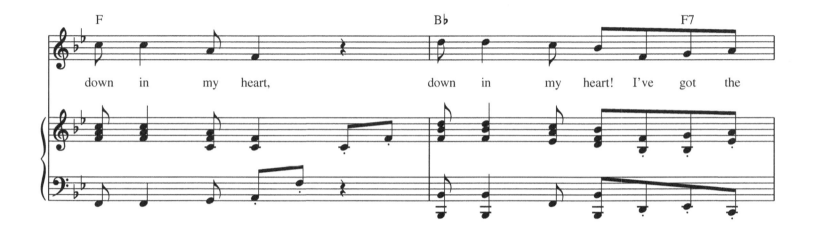

down in my heart, down in my heart! I've got the

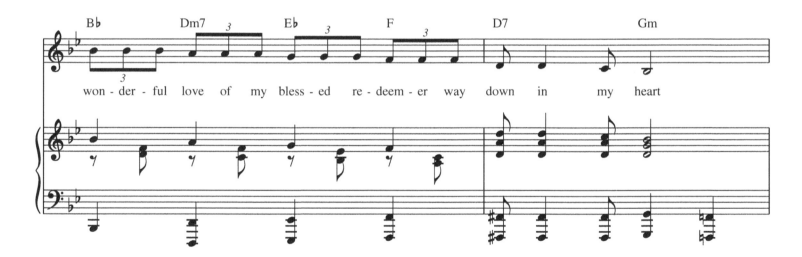

won-der-ful love of my bless-ed re-deem-er way down in my heart

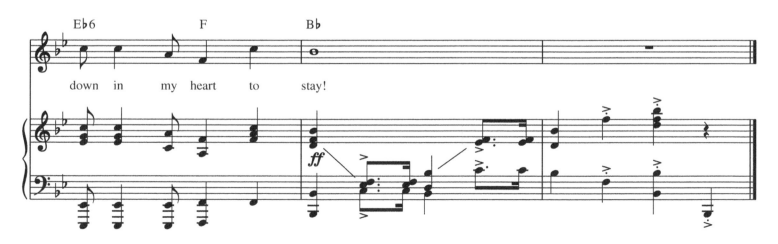

down in my heart to stay!

I WOULD BE TRUE

Words by HOWARD A. WALTER
Music by JOSEPH Y. PEEK

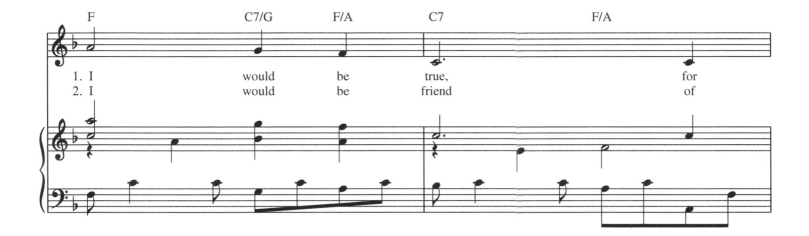

1. I would be true, for
2. I would be friend of

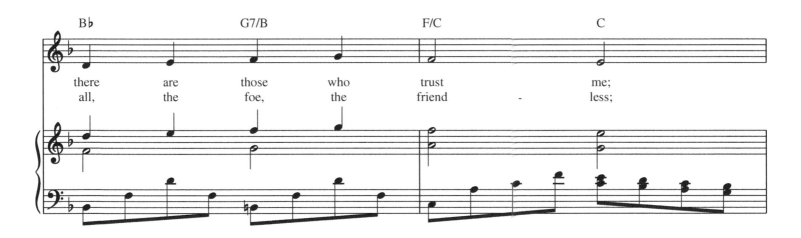

there are those who trust me;
all, are the those foe, who the trust friend - less;

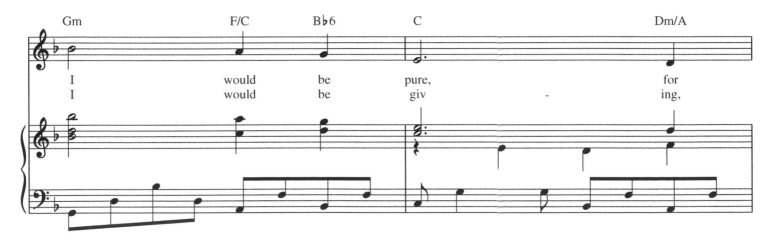

I would be pure, for
would be giv - ing,

there are those who care;
and for - get who the gift;

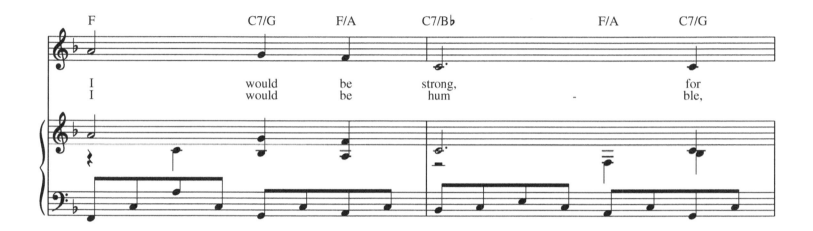

I would be strong, for
I would be hum - ble,

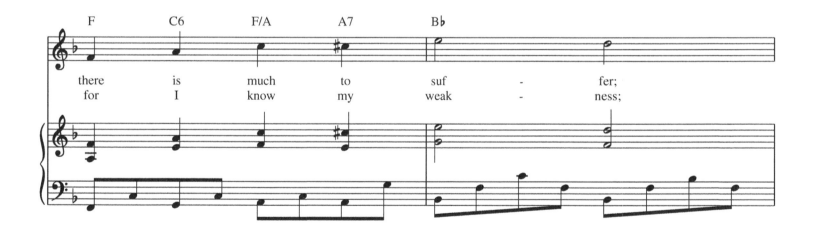

there is much to suf - fer;
for I know my weak - ness;

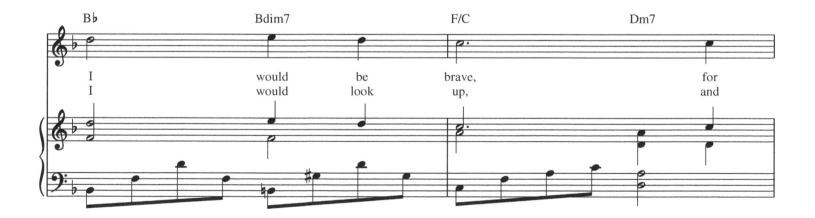

I would be brave, for
I would look up, and

there is much to dare,
laugh and love and live,

I would be brave, for
I would look up, and

there is much to dare.
laugh and love and live.

I'M IN THE LORD'S ARMY

Traditional

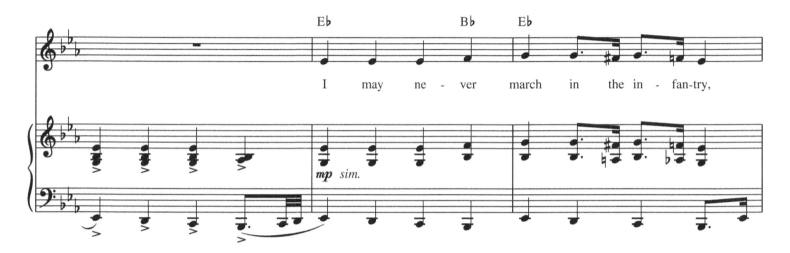

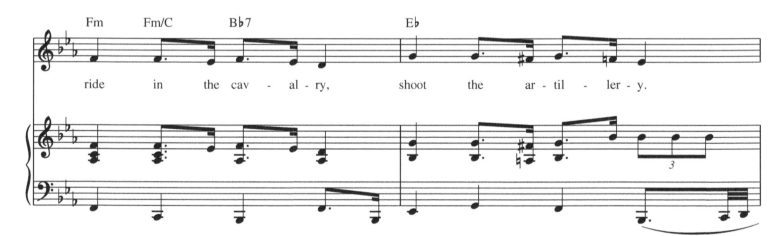

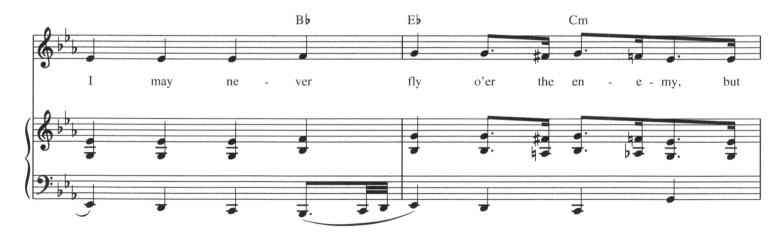

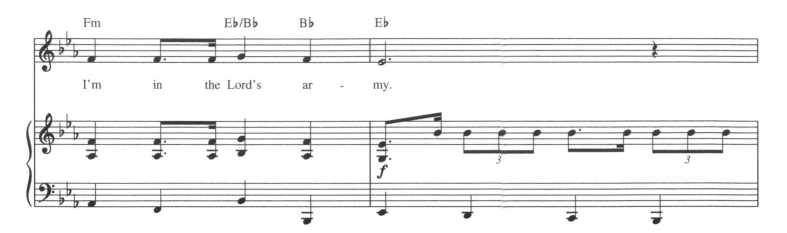

I'm in the Lord's ar - my.

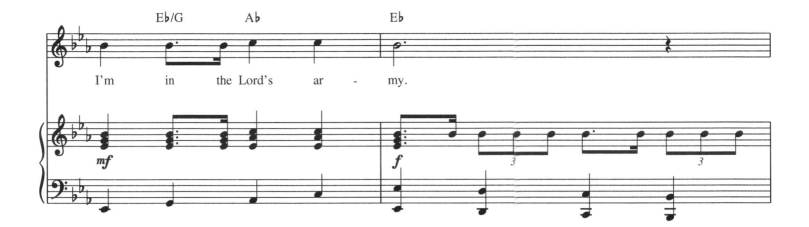

I'm in the Lord's ar - my.

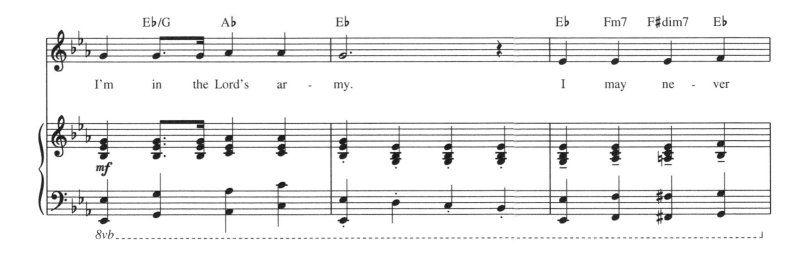

I'm in the Lord's ar - my. I may ne - ver

march in the in - fan - try, ride in the cav - al - ry,

JACOB'S LADDER

African-American Spiritual

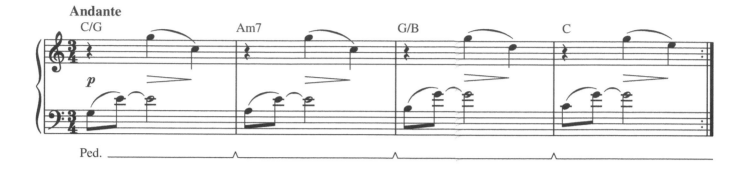

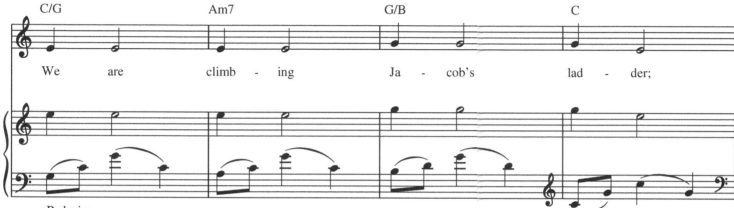

We are climb - ing Ja - cob's lad - der;

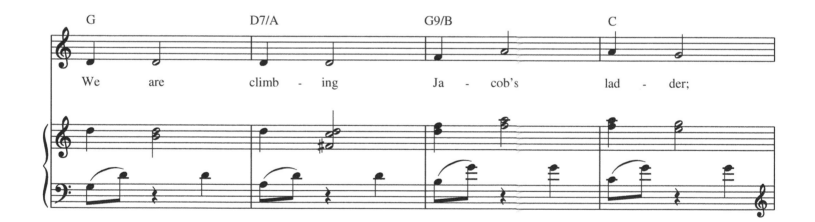

We are climb - ing Ja - cob's lad - der;

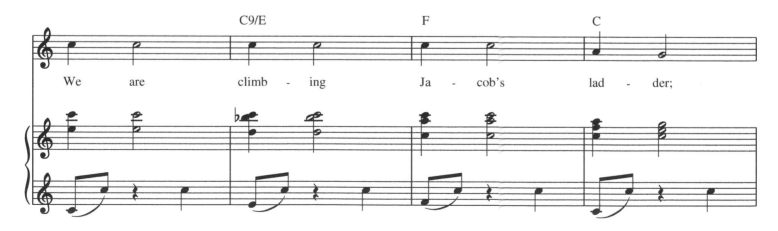

We are climb - ing Ja - cob's lad - der;

Sol - diers of the cross.

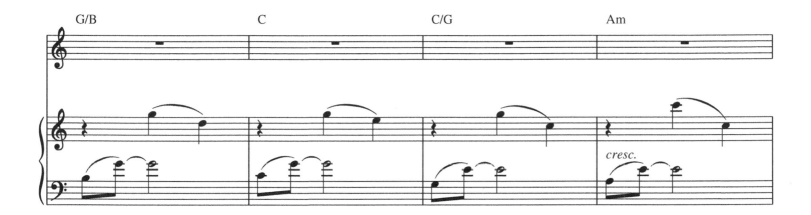

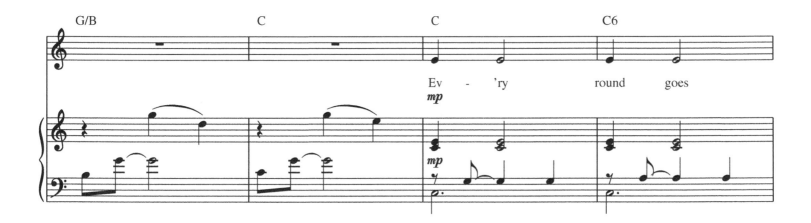

Ev - 'ry round goes

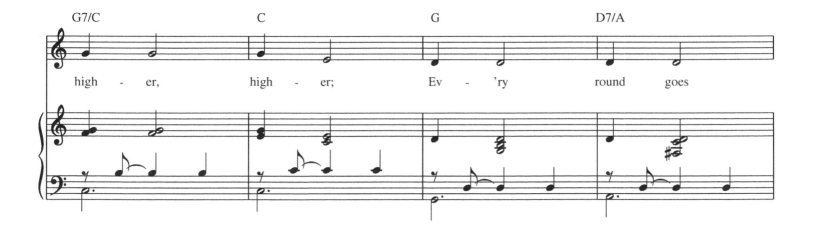

high - er, high - er; Ev - 'ry round goes

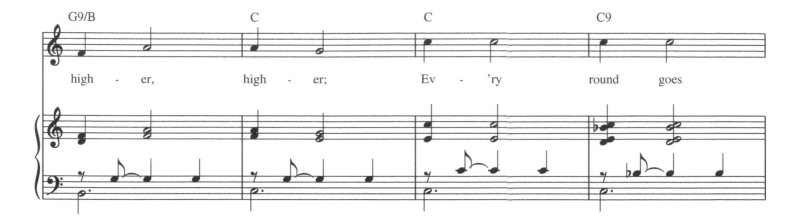

high - er,   high - er;   Ev - 'ry   round   goes

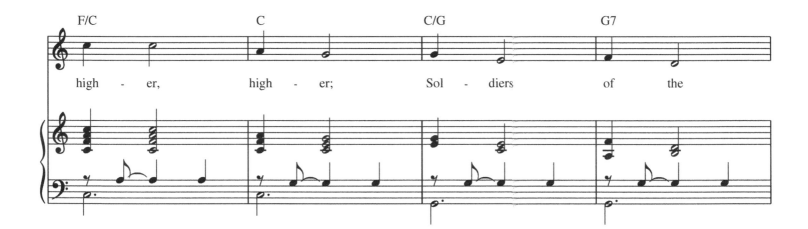

high - er,   high - er;   Sol - diers   of   the

cross.

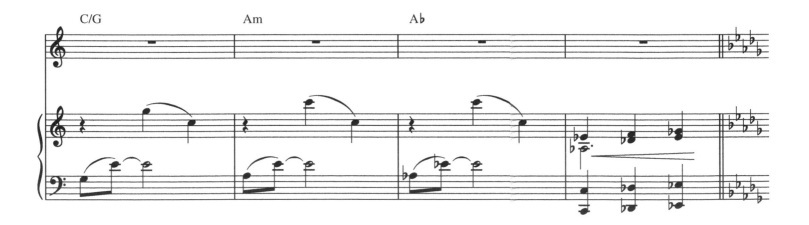

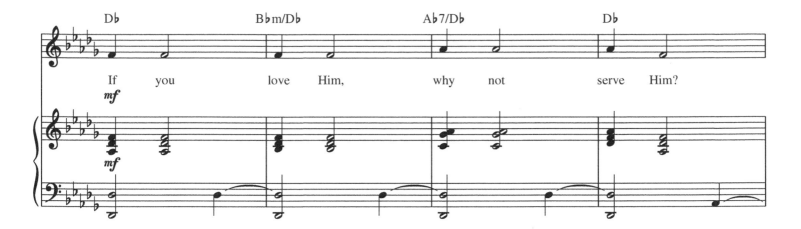

If you love Him, why not serve Him?

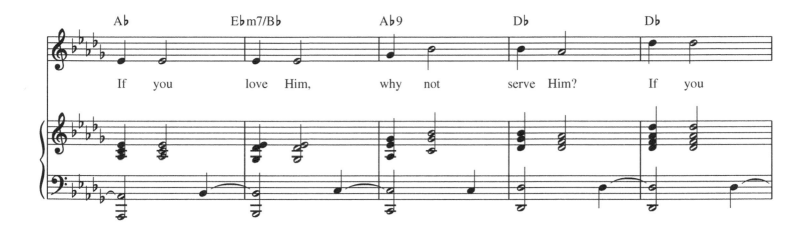

If you love Him, why not serve Him? If you

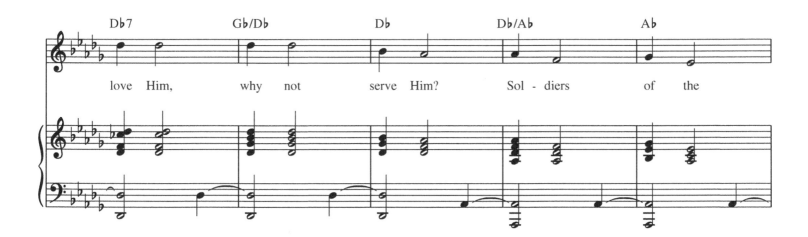

love Him, why not serve Him? Sol - diers of the

cross. We are climb - ing

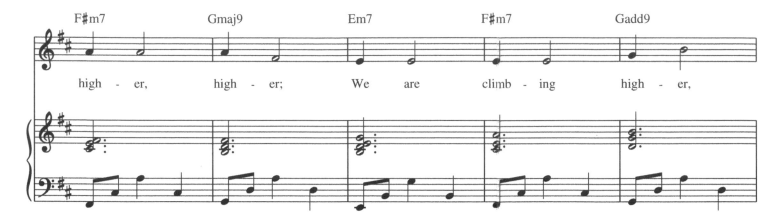

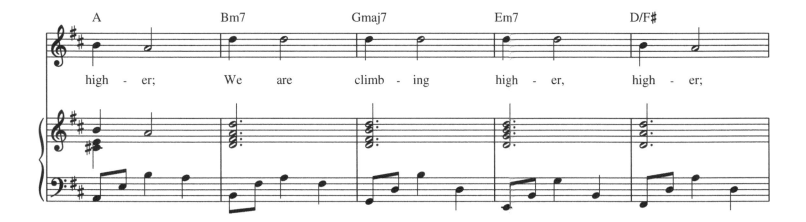

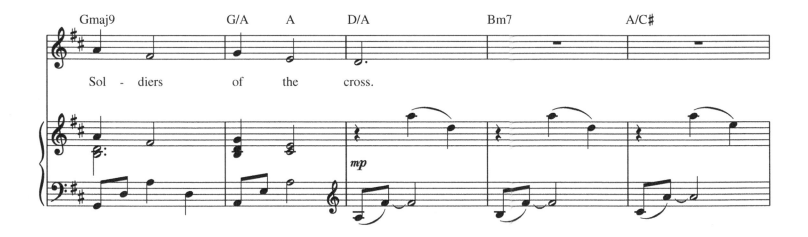

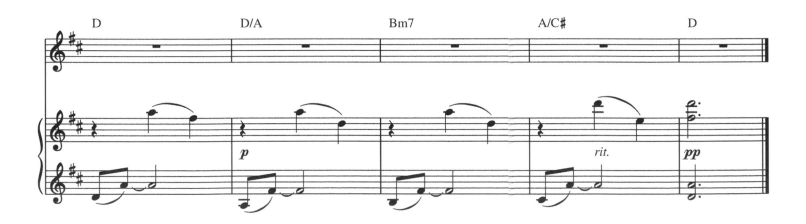

O, HOW I LOVE JESUS

Words by FREDERICK WHITFIELD
Traditional American Melody

Liltingly, in one

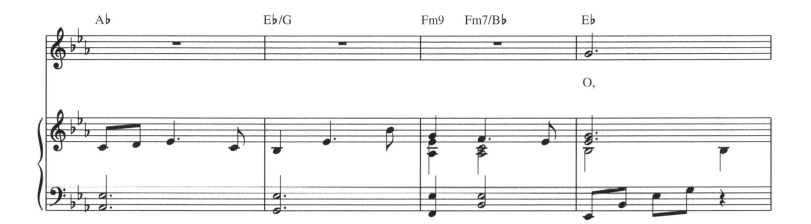

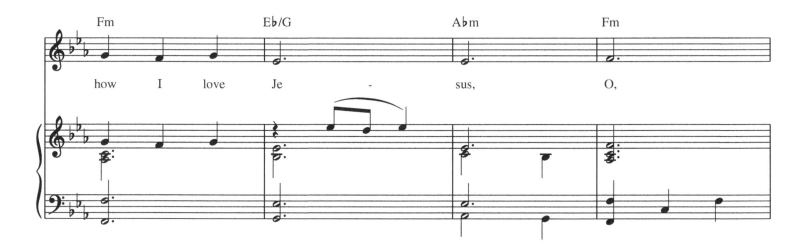

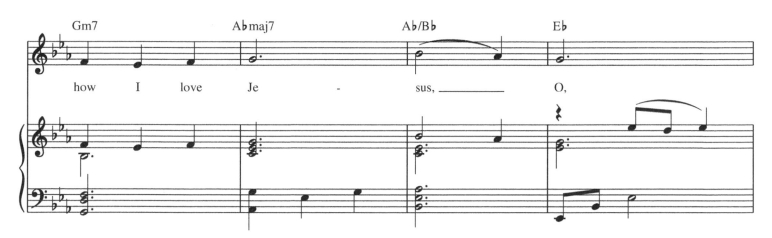

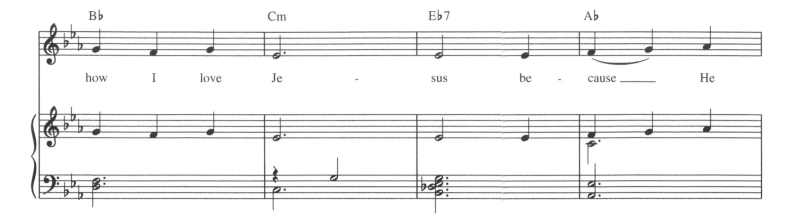

how I love Je - sus be - cause _____ He

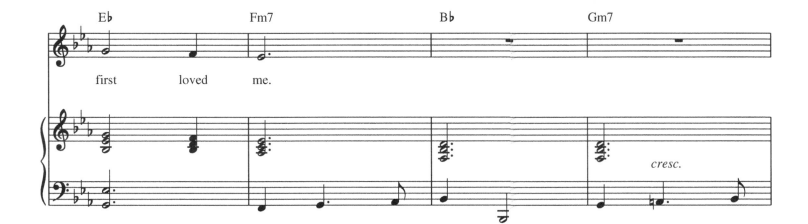

first loved me.

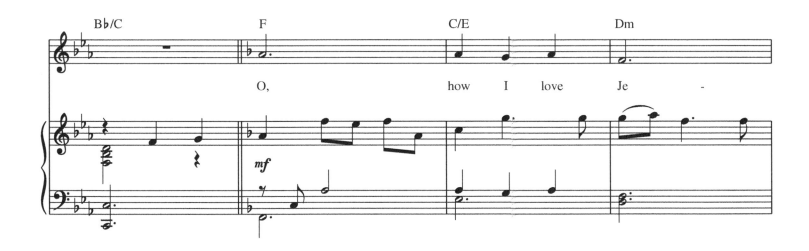

O, how I love Je -

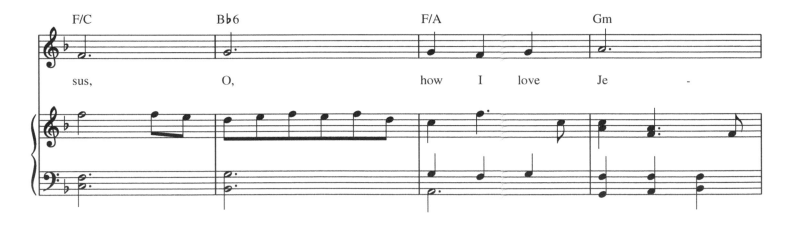

sus, O, how I love Je -

sus, _____ O, how I love Je -

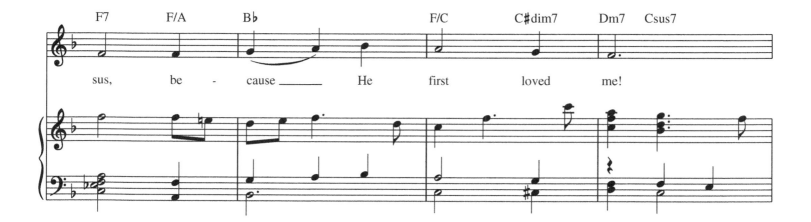

sus, be - cause _____ He first loved me!

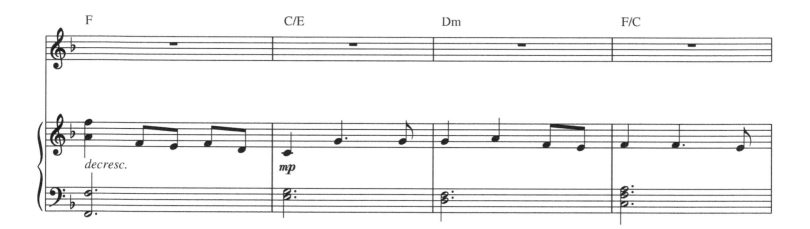

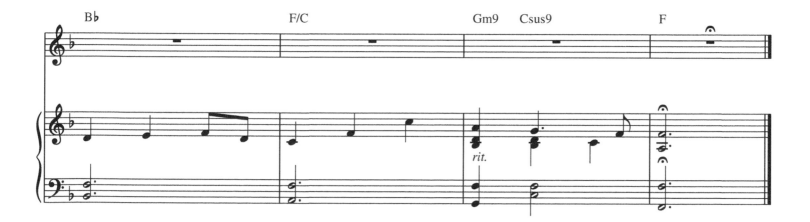

JESUS LOVES ME

Words by ANNA WARNER
Music by WILLIAM BRADBURY

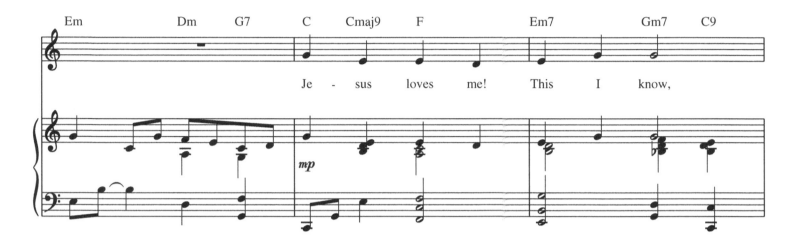

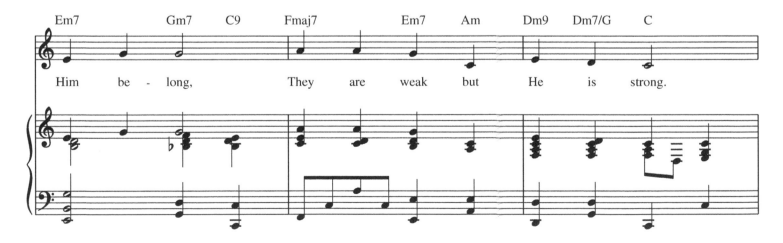

Yes, Je - sus loves me! Yes, Je - sus

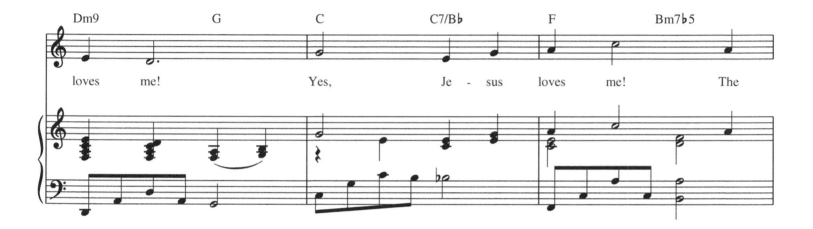

loves me! Yes, Je - sus loves me! The

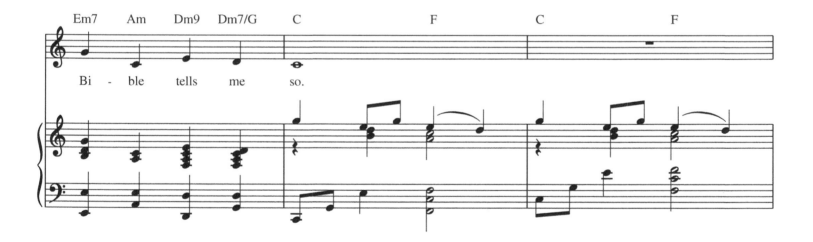

Bi - ble tells me so.

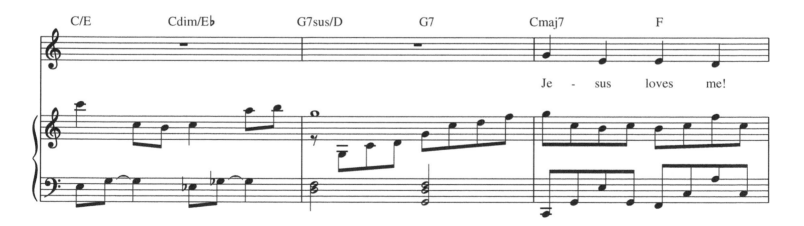

Je - sus loves me!

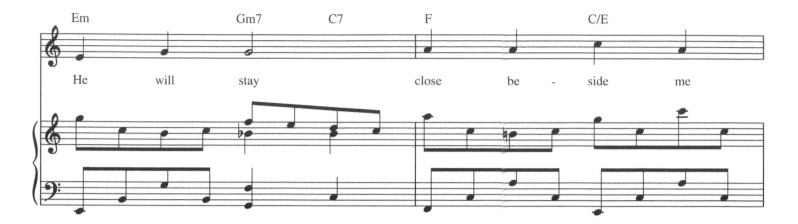

He will stay close be - side me

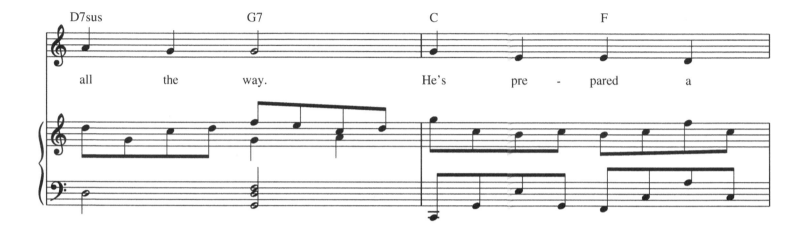

all the way. He's pre - pared a

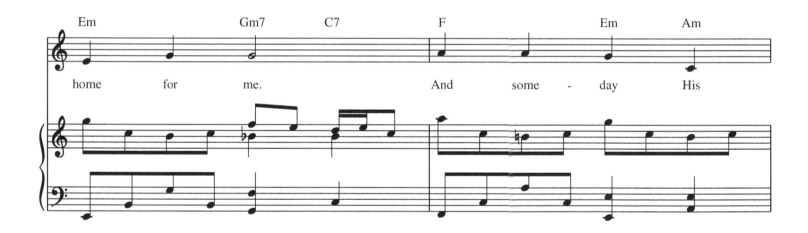

home for me. And some - day His

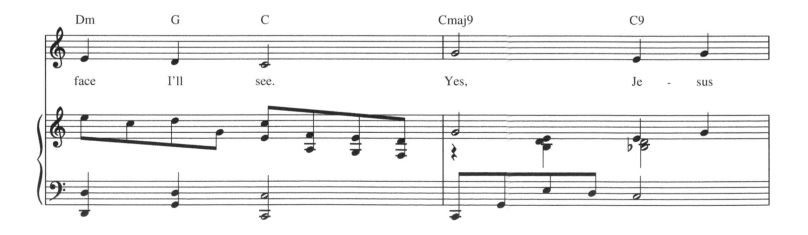

face I'll see. Yes, Je - sus

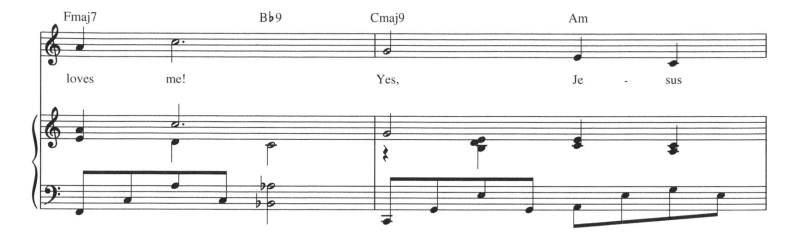

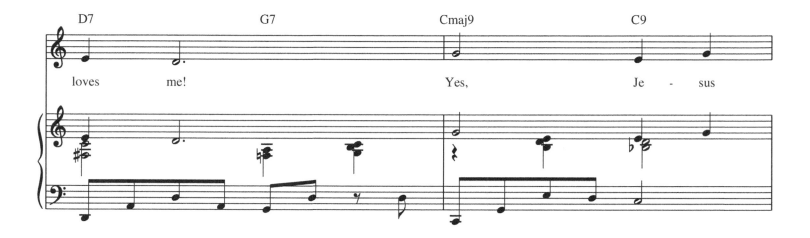

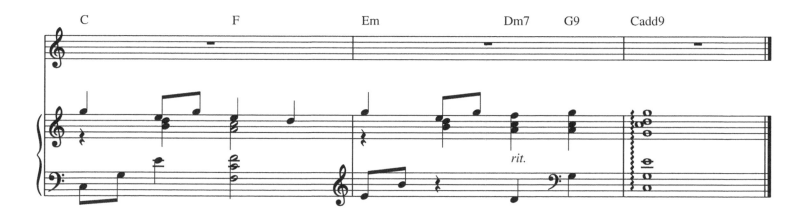

JESUS LOVES THE LITTLE CHILDREN

Traditional

chil - dren,   All   the   chil - dren of   the   world. _____   Red   and

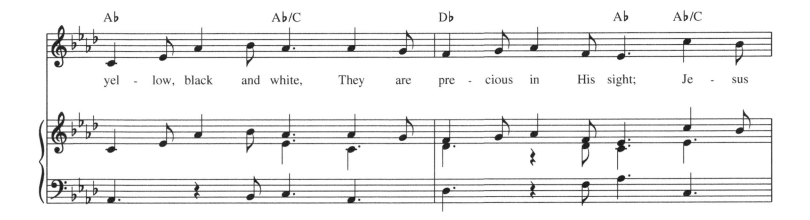

yel - low, black   and white,   They   are   pre - cious   in   His   sight;   Je - sus

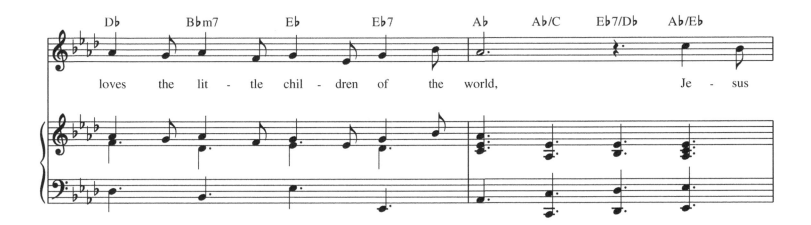

loves   the   lit - tle   chil - dren   of   the   world,   Je - sus

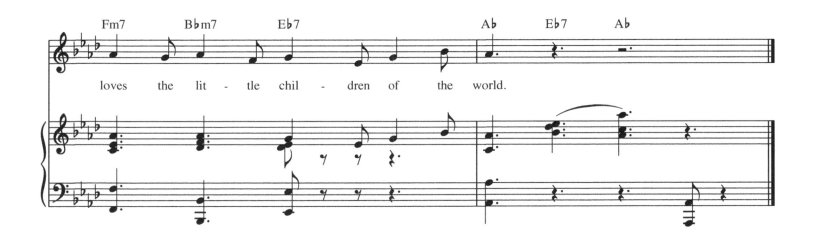

loves   the   lit - tle   chil - dren   of   the   world.

JUST AS I AM

Words by CHARLOTTE ELLIOTT
Music by WILLIAM BRADBURY

Expressively, in 1

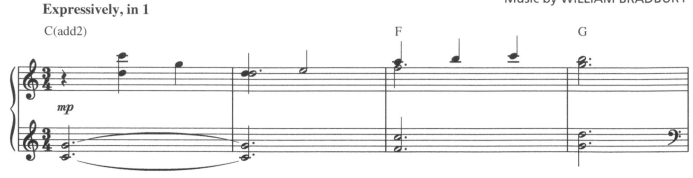

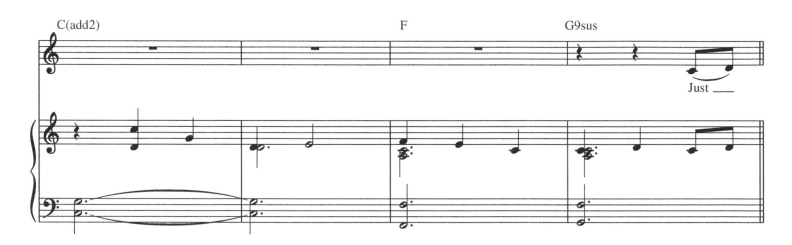

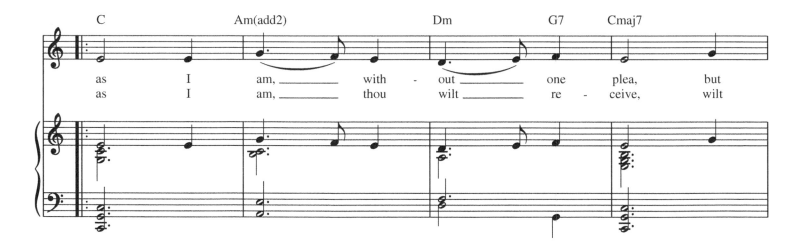

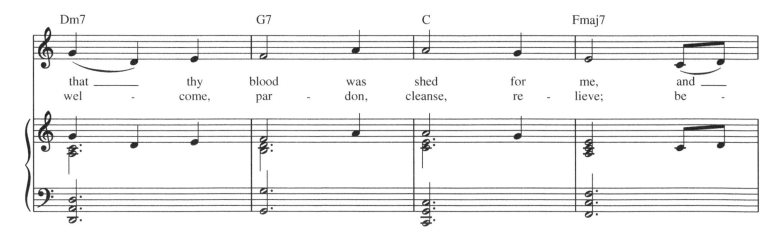

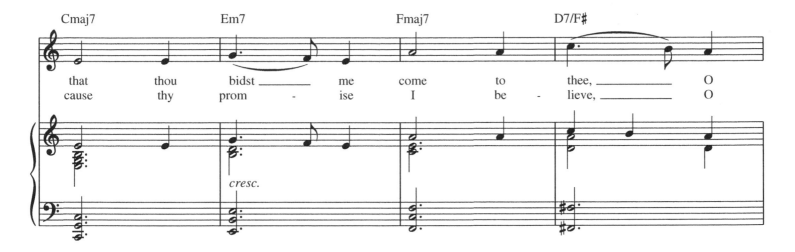

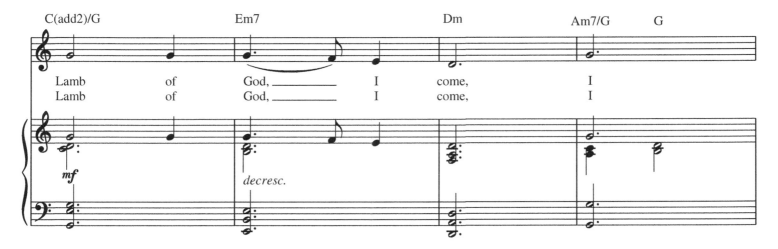

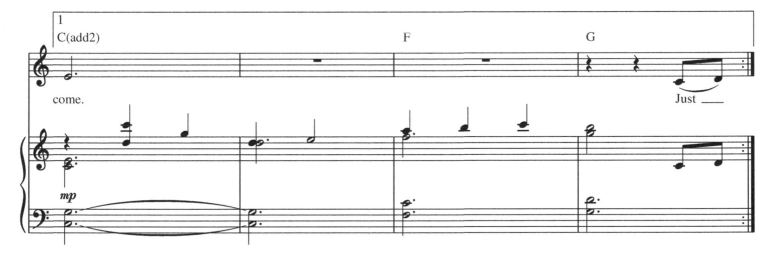

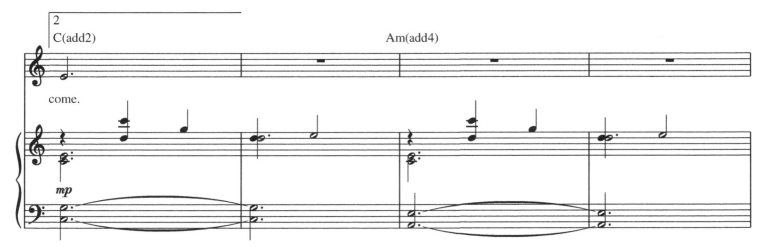

Slightly slower

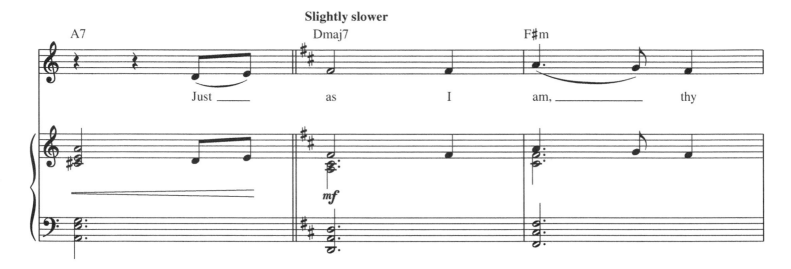

Just _____ as I am, _____ thy

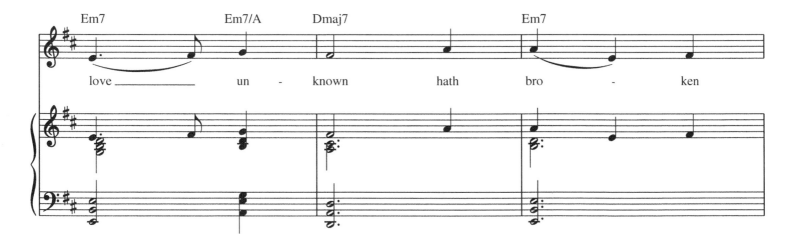

love _____ un - known hath bro - ken

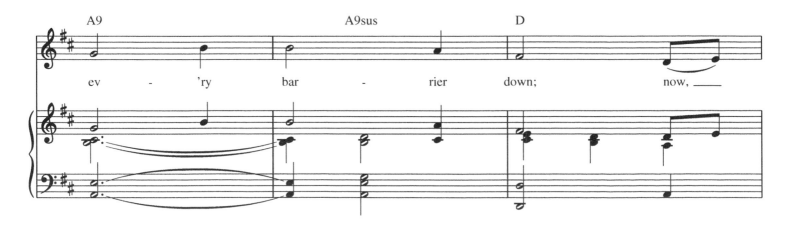

ev - 'ry bar - rier down; now, _____

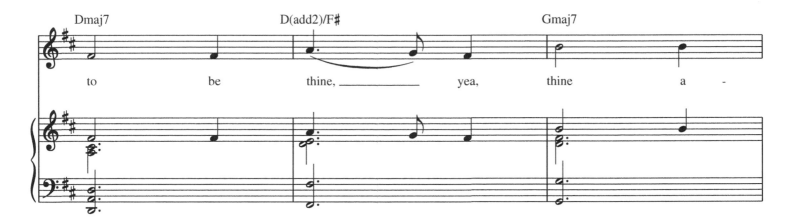

to be thine, _____ yea, thine a -

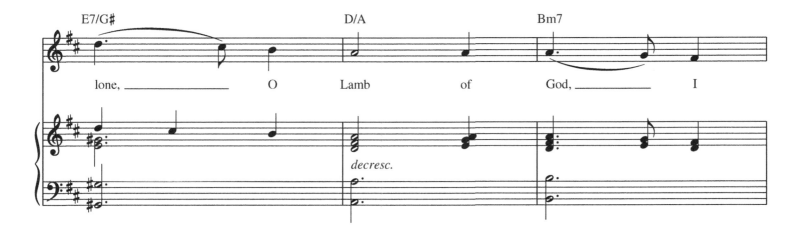

lone, _____ O Lamb of God, _____ I

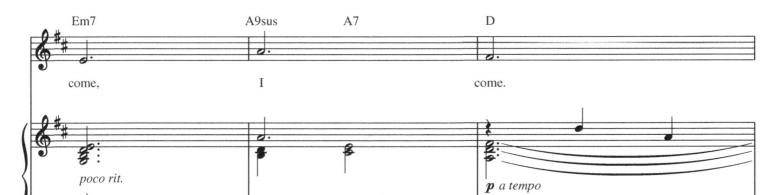

come, I come.

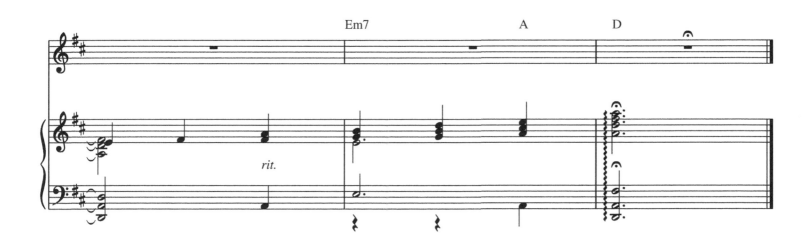

TELL ME THE STORIES OF JESUS

Traditional

Moderately

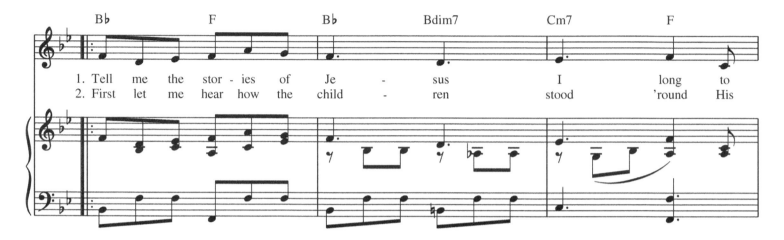

1. Tell me the stor-ies of Je - sus I long to
2. First let me hear how the child - ren stood 'round to His

hear;   Things I would ask Him to tell me
knee,   And I shall fan-cy His bless - ing

if He were here: Scenes by the
rest - ing on me;   Words full of

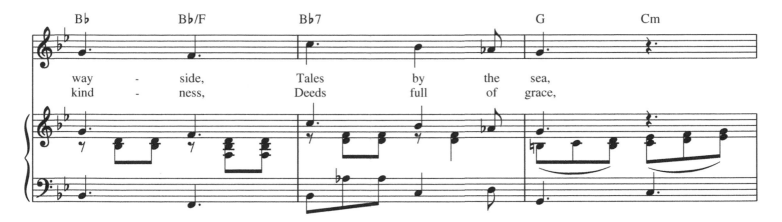

way - side, Tales by the sea,
kind - ness, Deeds full of grace,

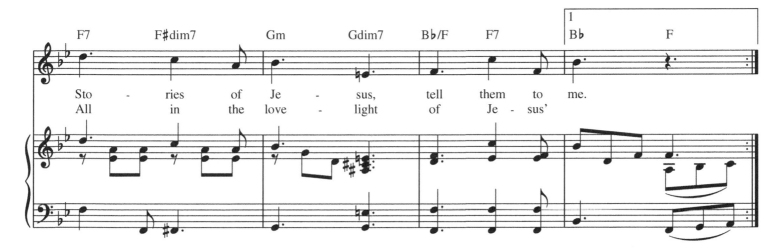

Sto - ries of Je - sus, tell them to me.
All in the love - light of Je - sus'

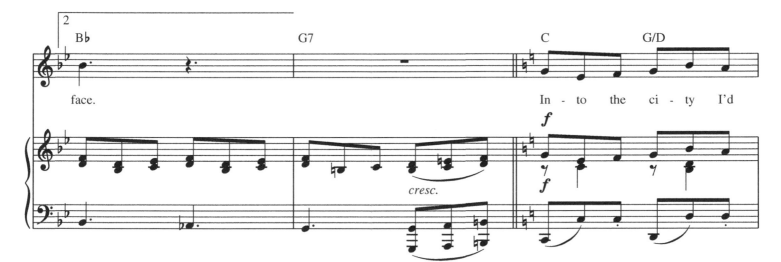

face.   In - to the ci - ty I'd

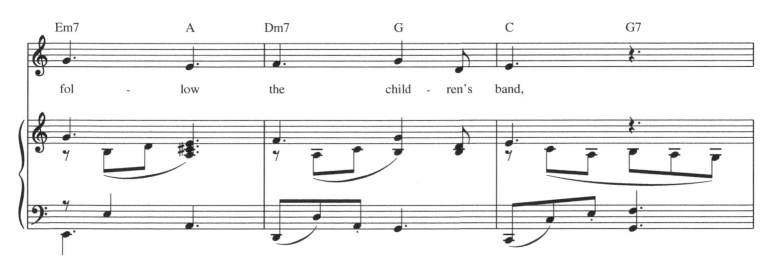

fol - low the child - ren's band,

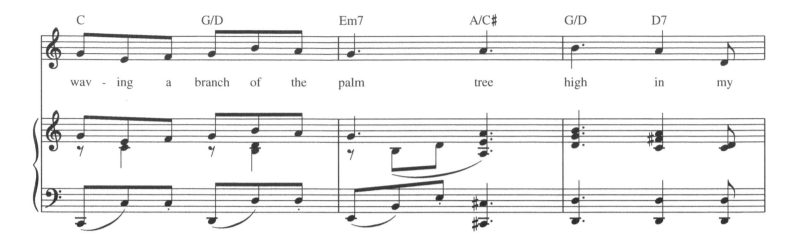

wav - ing a branch of the palm tree high in my

hand; One of His her - alds,

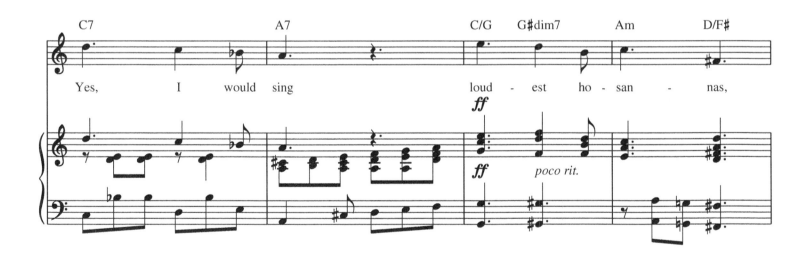

Yes, I would sing loud - est ho - san - nas,

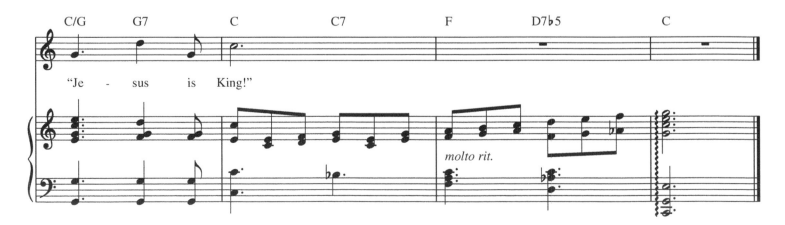

"Je - sus is King!"

THIS IS MY FATHER'S WORLD

Words by MALTBIE BABCOCK
Music by FRANKLIN L. SHEPPARD

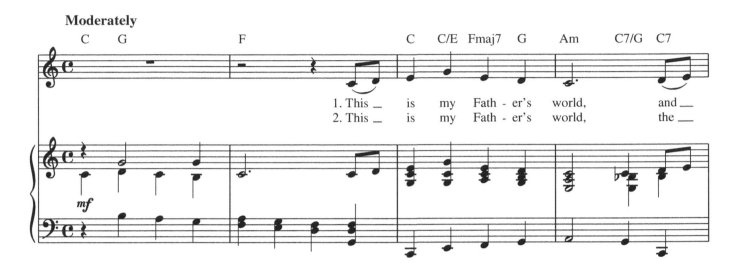

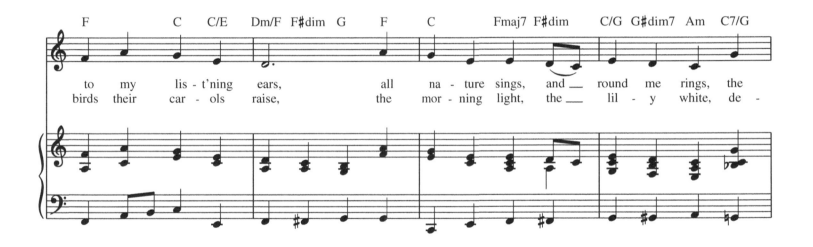

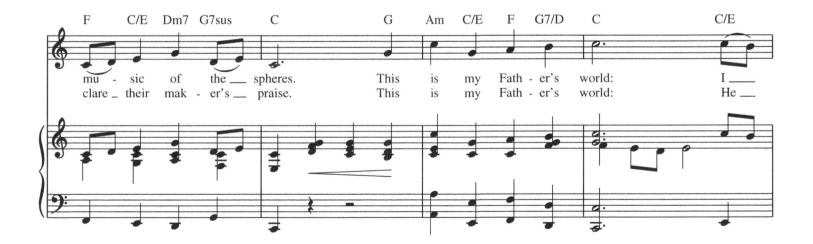

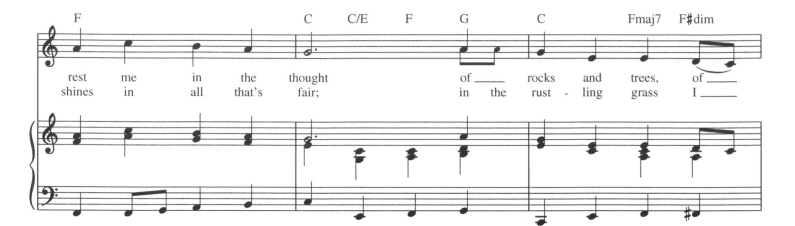

rest me in the thought of ____ rocks and trees, of ____
shines in all that's fair; in the rust - ling grass I ____

skies and seas; His hand __ the won - ders __ wrought.
hear him pass; He speaks _ to me ev - 'ry - where.

This __ is my Fath - er's world. O ____

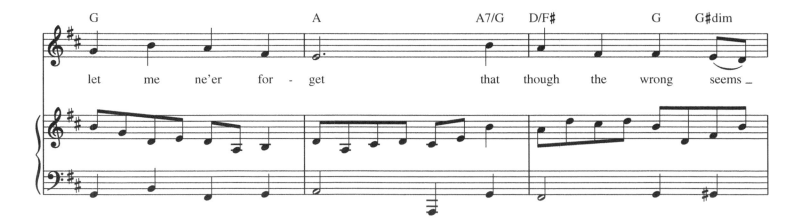

let me ne'er for - get that though the wrong seems __

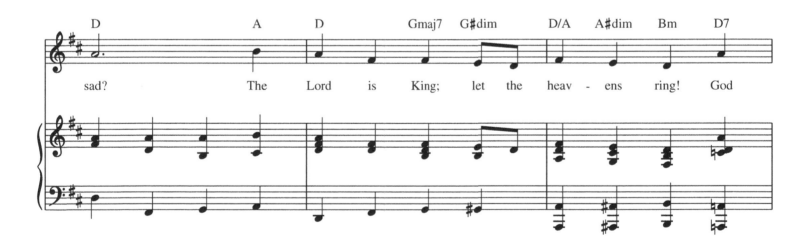

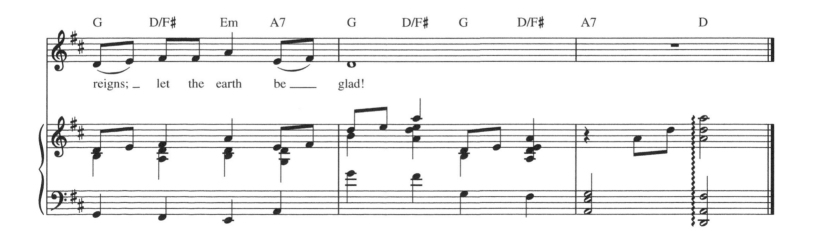

THIS LITTLE LIGHT OF MINE

African-American Spiritual

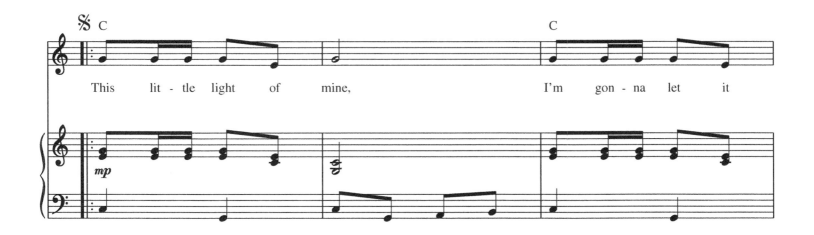

This lit-tle light of mine, I'm gon-na let it

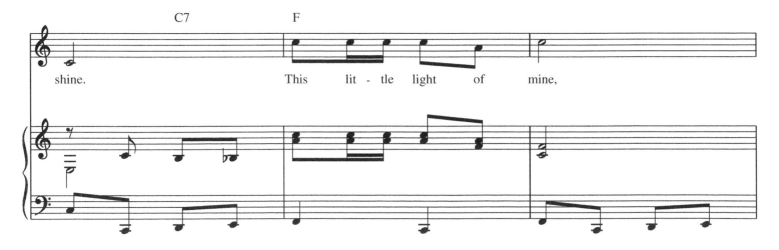

shine. This lit-tle light of mine,

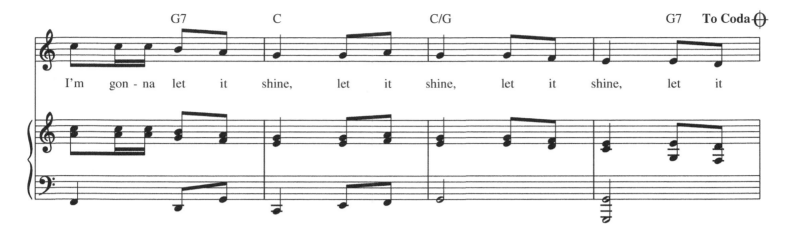

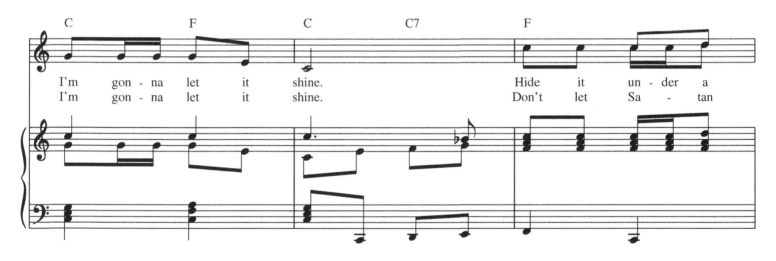

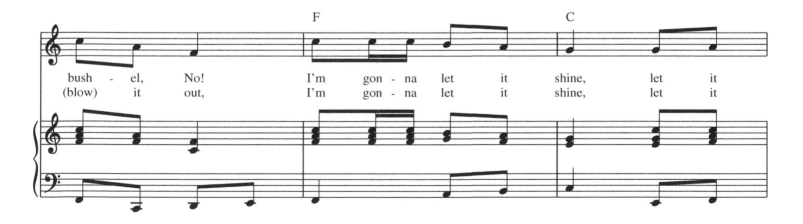

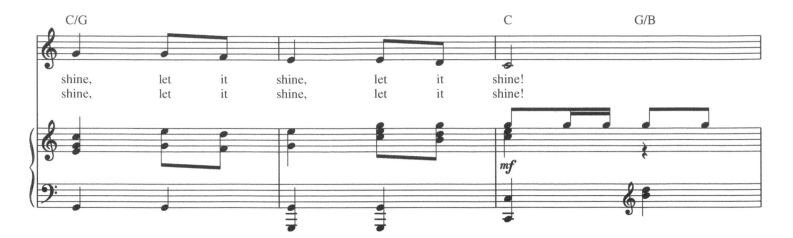

shine, let it shine, let it shine!
shine, let it shine, let it shine!

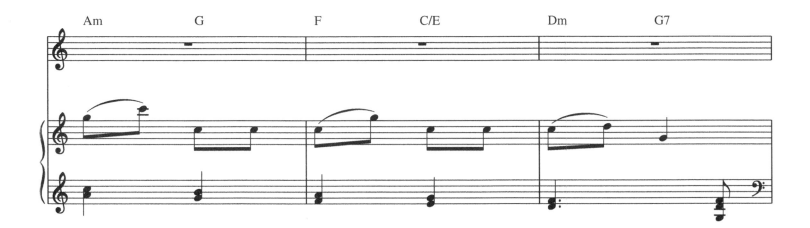

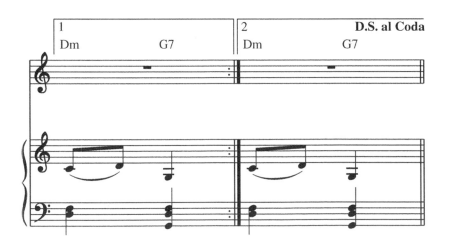

D.S. al Coda

CODA

shine!

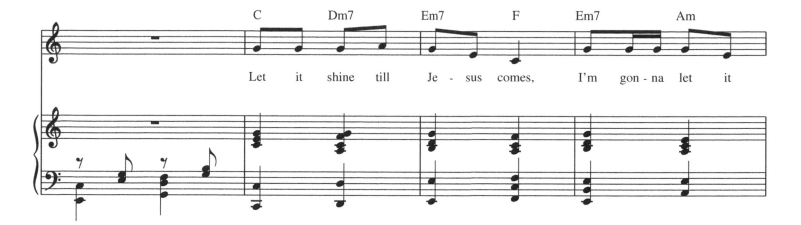

Let it shine till Je - sus comes, I'm gon - na let it

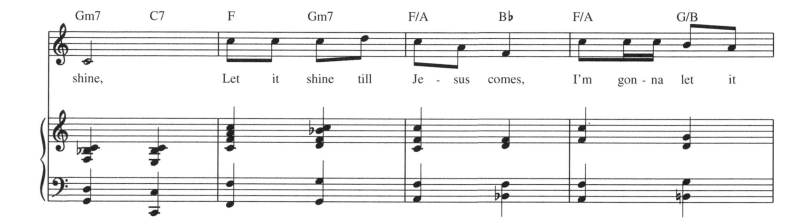

shine, Let it shine till Je - sus comes, I'm gon - na let it

shine, let it shine, let it shine, let it shine! _____

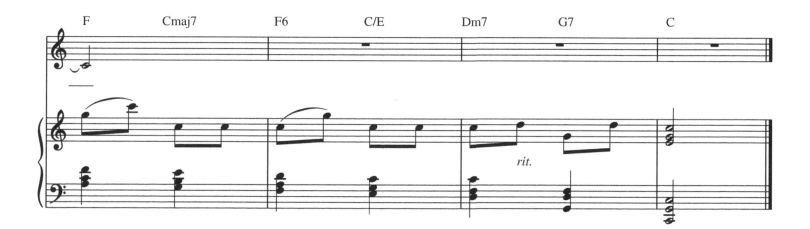

TRUST AND OBEY

Words by JOHN H. SAMMIS
Music by DANIEL B. TOWNER

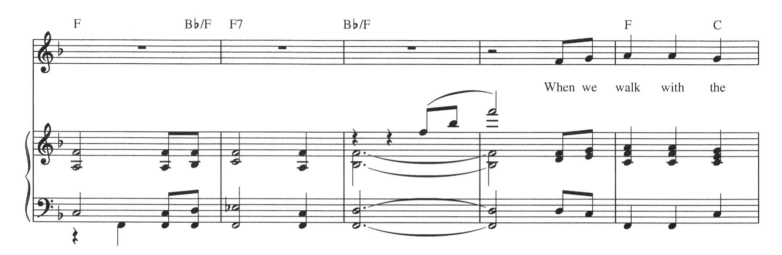

When we walk with the

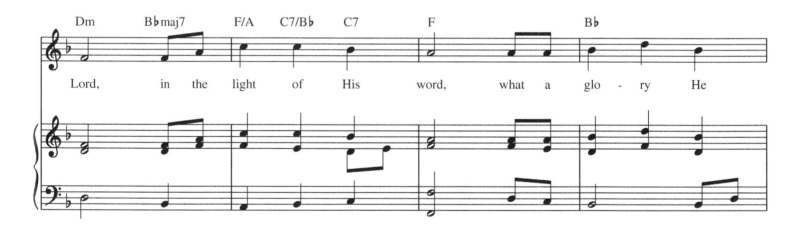

Lord, in the light of His word, what a glo-ry He

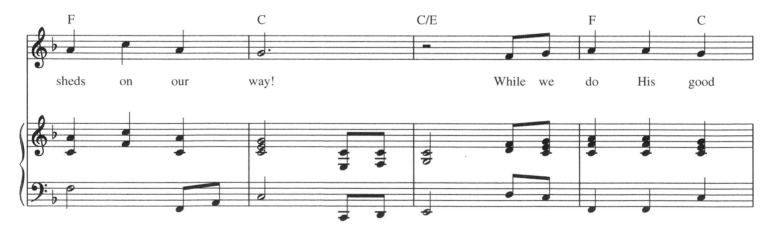

sheds on our way! While we do His good

will, He a- bides with us still, and with all who will

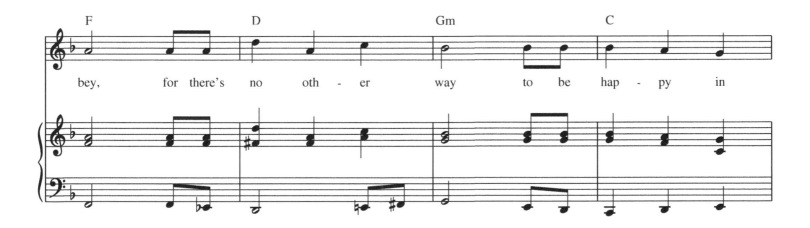

trust and o - bey. Trust and o -

bey, for there's no oth - er way to be hap - py in

Je - sus, _____ but to trust and o - bey.

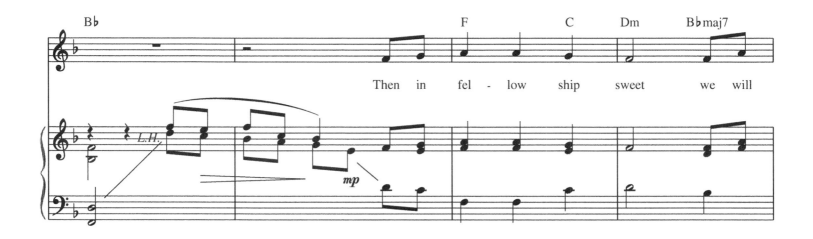

Then in fel - low ship sweet we will

sit at His feet, or we'll walk by His side in the

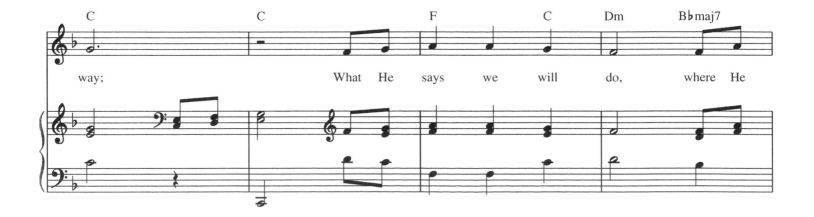

way; What He says we will do, where He

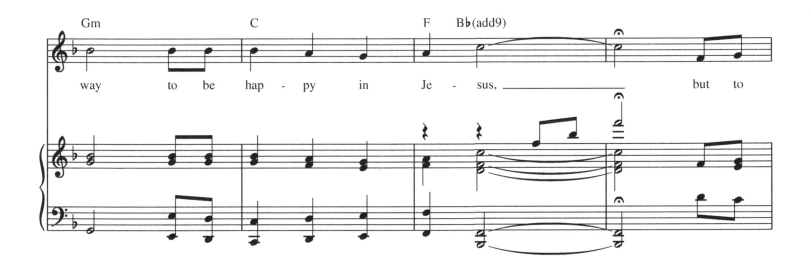

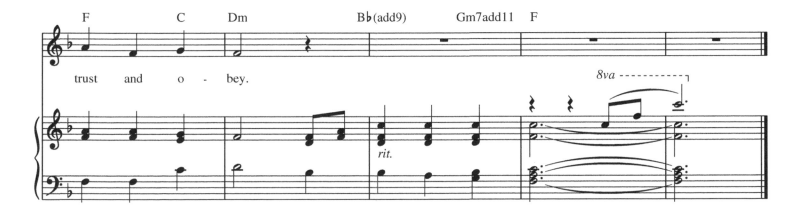

ZACCHAEUS

Traditional

Steady; lightly and crisply

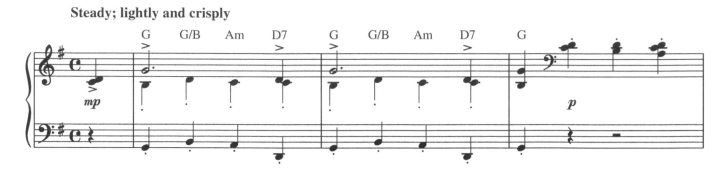

Zac-chae-us was a wee lit-tle man, and a wee lit-tle man was he. He climbed up in a syc-a-more tree, for the

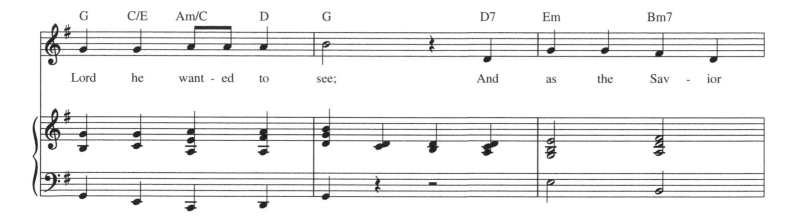

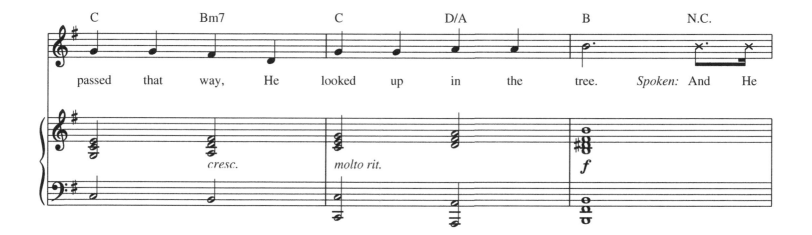

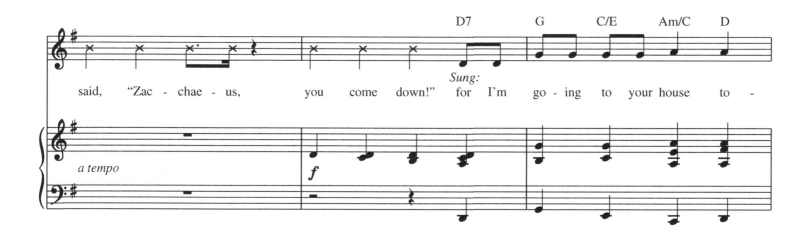

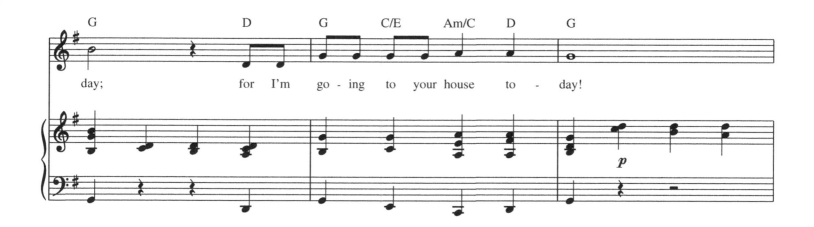

50

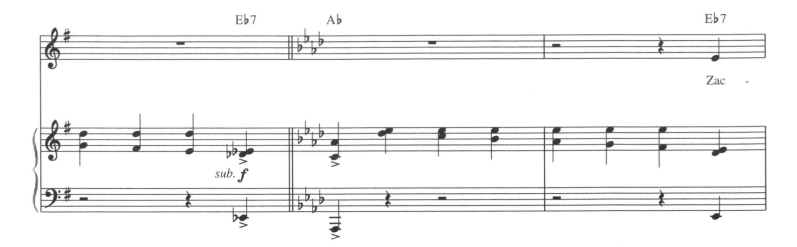

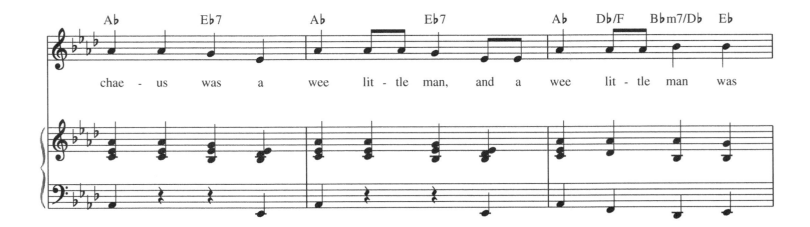

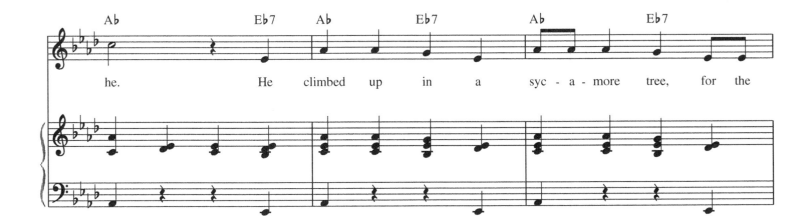

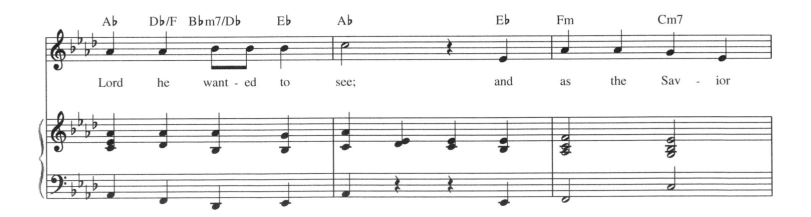

passed that way, He looked up in that tree.

Spoken: "Come on down!" *Sung:* for I'm go-ing to your house to-day, for I'm

go-ing to your house to-day! For I'm go-ing to your house to-

day! To-day!

WHAT A FRIEND WE HAVE IN JESUS

Words by JOSEPH SCRIVEN
Music by CHARLES C. CONVERSE

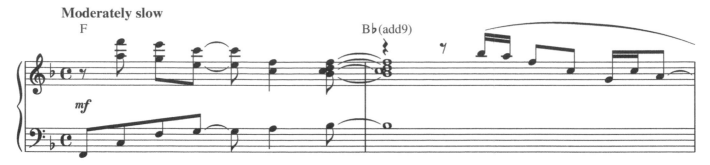

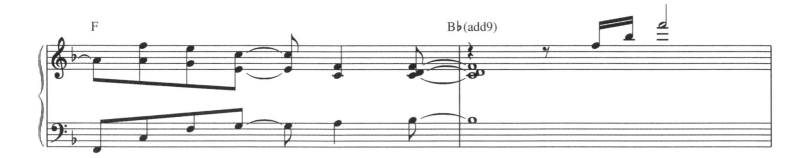

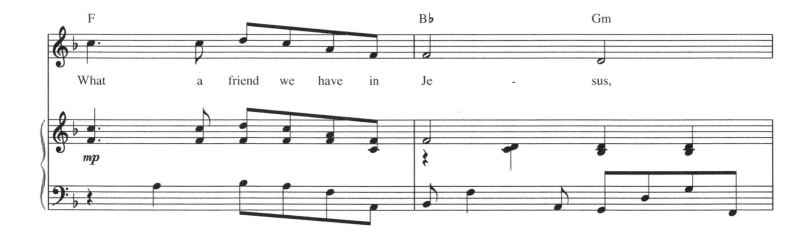

What a friend we have in Je - sus,

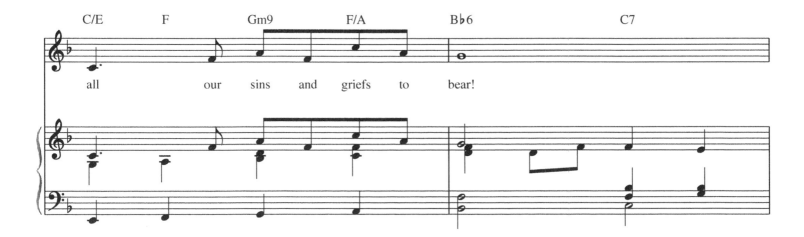

all our sins and griefs to bear!

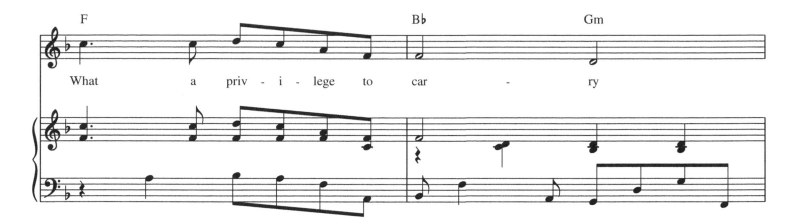

What a priv - i - lege to car - - - ry

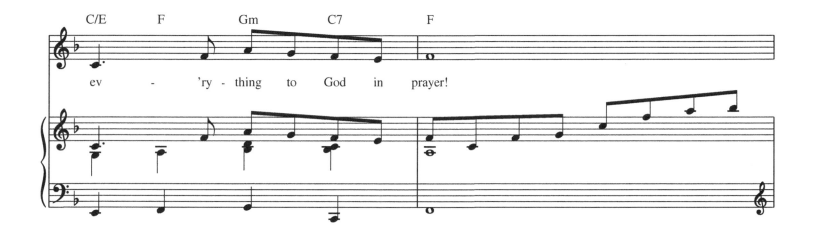

ev - - 'ry - thing to God in prayer!

O, what peace we of - ten for - - feit,

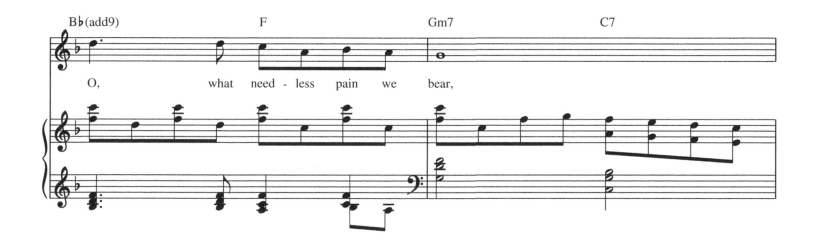

O, what need - less pain we bear,

all be - cause we do not car - ry

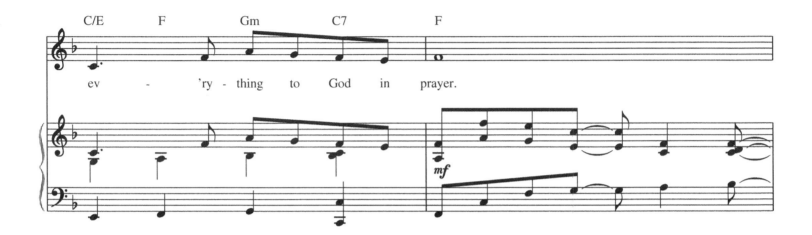

ev - 'ry - thing to God in prayer.

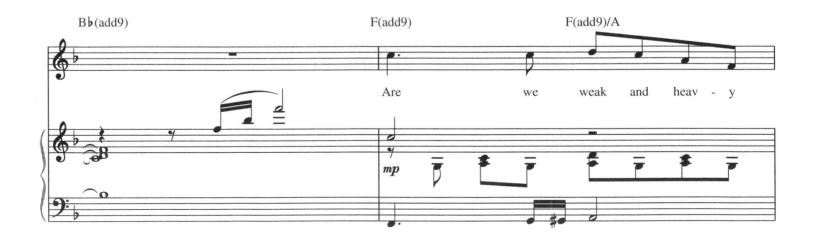

Are we weak and heav - y

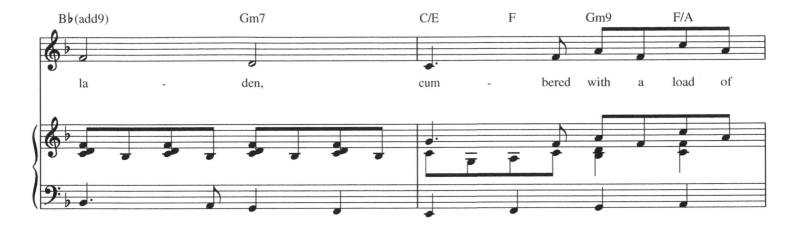

la - den, cum - bered with a load of

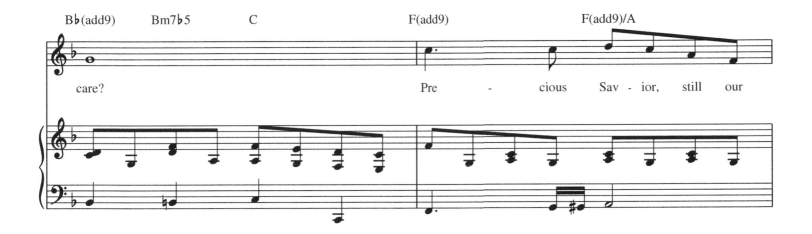

care? Pre - cious Sav - ior, still our

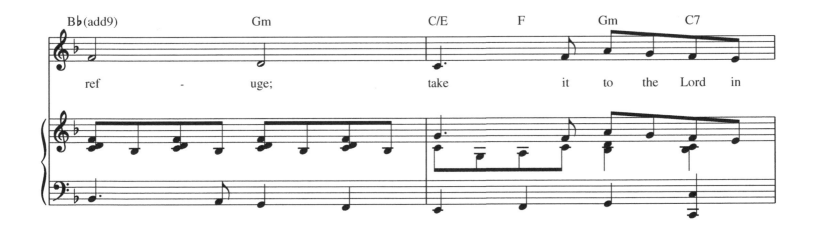

ref - uge; take it to the Lord in

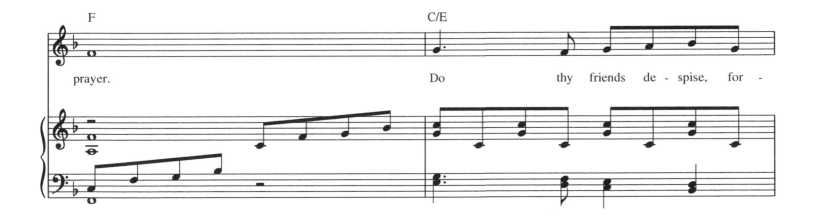

prayer. Do thy friends de - spise, for -

sake thee? Take it to the Lord in

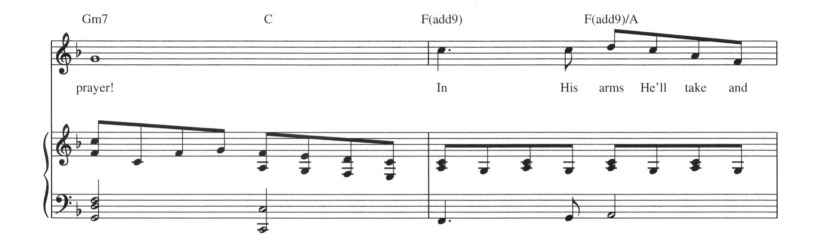

prayer! In His arms He'll take and

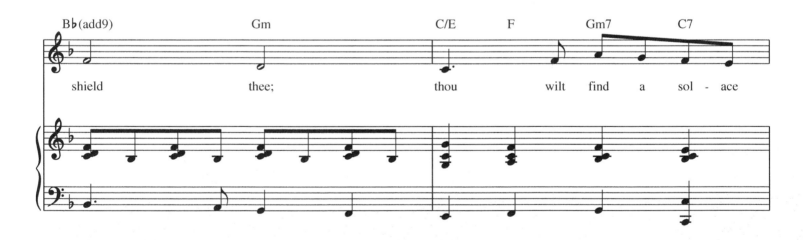

shield thee; thou wilt find a sol - ace

there.